Authentic
EGYPTIAN COOKING

Authentic
EGYPTIAN COOKING

From the Table of Abou El Sid

Nehal Leheta

The American University in Cairo Press
Cairo   New York

This paperback edition published in 2020 by
The American University in Cairo Press
113 Sharia Kasr el Aini, Cairo, Egypt
One Rockefeller Plaza, New York, NY 10020
www.aucpress.com

Dar el Kutub No. 7996/20
ISBN 978 977 679 004 9

Dar el Kutub Cataloging-in-Publication Data

Leheta, Nehal
    Authentic Egyptian Cooking from the Table of Abou El Sid /
Nehal Leheta.—Cairo: The American University in Cairo Press, 2020.
        p.   cm.
    ISBN 978 977 679 004 9
    1.Cooking—Egyptian
    641.5962

1 2 3 4 5   24 23 22 21 20

Photography by Sherif Tamim
Food styling by Hoda El-Sherif
Food styling and photography coordination by Rana Sarrouf
Opposite page photograph by Karim El Hayawan
Designed by **equinox**graphics*

Printed in China

contents

Introduction to Abou El Sid

Twice chosen by *Condé Nast Traveler* as one of the top fifty new restaurants in the world, and four-time winner of the Egyptian Ministry of Tourism Award for Excellence, Abou El Sid is celebrated for its rich mélange of Egyptian flavors and its unique fusion of cuisine, décor, lighting, and music that conjure an Egypt of the golden age from the 1920s to the 1950s. Founded in 2000, decorated with renowned artist Chant Avedissian's Cairo Stencil collection, and echoing to the classic music of Umm Kulthum, Farid al-Atrash, and Abdel Wahab, this favorite Cairo restaurant serves the best of traditional Egyptian dishes rarely found outside private homes.

The restaurant is named for the fictional character of Abou El Sid, who once upon a time was famous for his hospitality, his generosity, and his legendary cooking. News of his exquisite Egyptian meals— delicacies such as *fuul* with *tahina*, *koshari*, stuffed pigeons with rice, *molokheya* with rabbit, *fiteer meshaltet*—spread from his neighbors to the sultan, who asked him to come and cook for him at his palace. But while this was a great honor, Abou El Sid tired of the palace and soon returned home, to his preferred place among the common people of Egypt, who loved his cuisine best, and continued to prepare with love the wholesome and delicious dishes of authentic Egyptian cooking.

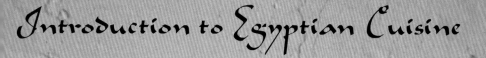

Introduction to Egyptian Cuisine

The ancient Egyptians left much evidence suggesting their love for a variety of food and feasts, and the illustrations in tomb and temple art suggest that much of ancient Egyptian cuisine has been preserved to the present day.

Although trade patterns and long centuries of foreign rule have naturally affected Egyptian cooking, the same core ingredients and general methods remain intact. Foreign influence, be it French, British, Greek, Turkish, Lebanese, or Syrian, has surprisingly resulted in only minor alterations to the taste and texture of the original dishes.

In Egypt we talk of *al-nafas fi-l-akl,* referring to a cook's personal touch and the idiosyncrasies, positive energy, and love that go into cooking. Each home has its own variation on every recipe. Eating at an Egyptian home is a new and delightful experience for someone from a different culture, often involving a large number of people, as sharing a meal is highly regarded as a social event. The everyday table is set like a celebration, full of different *mezza* (appetizers), main courses, rice, and bread. Families take their time over a meal, and it is part of the tradition for all to 'dig into' the food by dipping into the variety of different communal dishes with 'cat's ear' folds of the pita-like *shami* or *baladi* bread.

Egyptian cuisine is thus a splendid amalgamation of recipes showcasing the country's cosmopolitan and ancient heritage. It is a wonderful way in which a memory of Egypt's extraordinary past can be recollected.

Common Ingredients

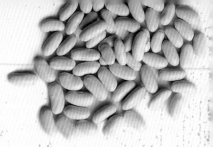

white beans

BURGHUL: cracked wheat, also known as bulgur.

CARDAMOM PODS: an aromatic spice native to Egypt. Its taste is strong and sweet.

CORIANDER POWDER: an herb of yellow granules, commonly used in Egyptian cuisine.

DITALINI PASTA: the specific kind of pasta used in *koshari*. It is shaped like a small hollow tube.

DRIED HOMOS: dried chickpeas or garbanzo beans.

FAVA BEANS: a type of broad bean plant, used to make *fuul*.

FIREEK: green wheat, with a crunchy texture, sometimes used as a substitute for rice. It is usually soaked in water for half an hour before cooking.

MIXED NUTS: Abou El Sid's mixed nuts are made up of raisins, almonds, and hazelnuts.

MIXED SPICES: a mixture of ground cloves, cinnamon, nutmeg, and pepper.

MOLOKHEYA: the leaves of the Corochorus species. It is known in English as Jew's mallow, jute mallow, or nalta. Not to be confused with mallow leaf. In Egypt, the fresh *molokheya* leaves are picked from the stems and then minced.

dried homos

OKRA: a vegetable in the mallow family.

ORZO: rice-shaped pasta; also called risoni.

cardamom pods

fava beans (fuul)

burghul

PEPPER: Abou El Sid uses three different types of pepper: black pepper, white pepper, and red chili pepper. White pepper has a milder flavor than black or red. Red chili pepper comes in a variety of different kinds: mild, sweet red pepper, paprika, and chili powder.

PINE NUTS: small edible seeds from pine.

RICE: Egyptians cook with short-grain white rice.

RISONI: see Orzo.

SAFFRON: a relatively expensive type of seasoning derived from a flower. It is used not only as a seasoning, but also to color foods like rice.

SALT: Abou El Sid uses coarsely ground salt for cooking.

SESAME SEED PASTE: used for making *tahina* paste. If ready-made *tahina* paste is not available, you can easily prepare it. Preheat the oven to 180°C. Toast sesame seeds in a pan in the oven until they change color, but don't let them get brown. Mix the toasted seeds in a blender with corn oil until the desired consistency is reached.

SHAAREYA: a type of vermicelli, very thin and short, sometimes used as a substitute for rice.

TAGIN: Arabic earthenware pot made of heavy clay, in which certain dishes are cooked.

shaareya

WHITE BEANS: a large bean (great northern beans) with a distinctive, delicate flavor.

WHOLE WHEAT GRAIN: uncrushed wheat grain.

orzo

13

soups

Chicken Soup with Orzo

Serves: 2 - 4 | Preparing the chicken soup: 40 minutes
Preparing the orzo: 5 minutes
Mixing: 10 minutes

Preparing the chicken soup

1. Heat oil and butter together in a saucepan.
2. Add grated onion, and sauté until it turns golden brown. Boil chicken breast for half an hour, and add chicken stock, salt, white pepper, bay leaf, and cardamom pod.
3. Add 1½ tsp flour and stir.

Preparing the orzo

4. Fry the orzo with a little corn oil in a pan until it turns golden brown.
5. Drain off the oil.
6. Add the orzo to the soup over medium heat, and boil for 10 min until the orzo expands.
7. Remove from heat.

Can be served with lemon juice.

2 tbsp corn oil

1 tsp butter

1 tbsp grated onion

1 chicken breast (about 100g / ¼ lb)

1 chicken stock cube, dissolved in 5 cups water

1 tsp salt

1 tsp white pepper

1 bay leaf

1 cardamom pod

225g / 1 cup orzo (also called risoni)

1½ tsp flour

juice of ½ lemon (optional)

_____

Orzo Chicken Soup is one of Egypt's most frequently served soups. It is known as shorbet lesan 'asfour. The origin of its name came from the shape of the orzo or risoni pasta. It is literally translated as 'bird's tongue.'

Lentil Soup

Serves: 2 - 4 | Preparation time: 30 minutes

1. Wash lentils well with water, and drain through a sieve.
2. Put lentils in a pan, add 3 cups of cold water, and heat.
3. Add grated carrots, sliced onions, and the 3 chopped garlic cloves to the lentils.
4. Add the potatoes, and mix together. Cook over medium heat for about 20 minutes. Remove from heat, and purée the mixture in a blender or food processor. Return the purée to the pan, heat, and stir in the butter. Season with salt and cumin.
5. If a thinner soup is wanted, add water; for a thicker texture, stir in flour.
6. In a different pan, sauté the 2 crushed garlic cloves with corn oil until they turn golden brown. Then add 1 tsp of crushed coriander leaves, and stir with the garlic. Add to the lentil soup; the hot mixture will make a "tshhhh" sound. This is known as *tasha* in Arabic.

Best served with toasted bread cut into 1-inch squares.

500g / 2 cups yellow lentils

300g / 4 carrots, grated

2 medium-sized onions (about 250g), sliced

5 garlic cloves—3 chopped, 2 crushed

1 medium potato (about 100g), peeled and grated

¼ tsp butter

½ tsp salt

¼ tsp cumin

4 tbsp corn oil

½ tbsp flour

1 tsp crushed coriander leaves

Lentil soup is an Egyptian favorite. It is highly nutritious, and often served with lemon wedges.

appetizers/mezze

Abou El Sid Eggplant Salad

Grilled Mashed Eggplant with Vegetables and Olive Oil

Serves: 2 - 4 | Preparation time: 25 minutes

1. Preheat oven to 260°C.
2. Wash the eggplant, green peppers, and tomatoes and dry well, leaving the skins on.
3. Poke the eggplant with a fork all over, then brush it with olive oil to help release its juices while cooking.
4. Chop the green peppers and tomatoes into small squares.
5. Put the eggplant, green pepper, and tomatoes in a pan and bake in the oven about 20 minutes, until the eggplant darkens and becomes tender.
6. Remove from oven and allow the vegetables to cool.
7. Peel and mash the baked eggplants, green pepper, and tomato in a bowl.
8. Add lemon juice to give it flavor, which also helps to preserve the eggplant's color.
9. Add minced garlic, olive oil, vinegar, salt, and chili to the bowl, and mix well.
10. Transfer to a serving plate.

Best served cold with Egyptian *baladi* bread (pita).

1 large eggplant (about 500g / 1 lb)

2 green peppers

2 medium tomatoes (about 300g)

juice of 1 lemon

1 garlic clove, minced

1 tbsp olive oil

1 tsp vinegar

½ tsp. salt

¼ tsp. chopped fresh chili

This recipe is made with eggplant, known in Egypt as bitingan roumi. It is baked like the baba ghanoug recipe. This salad is a special Egyptian vegetarian appetizer or mezza, served only at Abou El Sid restaurants.

Tahina

Sesame Cream Dip

Serves: 2 - 4 | Preparation Time: 5 minutes

1. Put *tahina* paste into the blender, and add the vinegar and lemon juice. Blend until well combined.
2. In a bowl, mix the warm water with the salt, chili, and cumin.
3. Add this to the *tahina* mixture and blend. If the mixture stiffens, continue with the blender on a low speed until it becomes creamy again.
4. Mince the garlic, stir it into the *tahina*, and drizzle olive oil over the top. Serve with small pieces of *baladi* bread or pita bread.

250ml / 1 cup *tahina* paste

1 tbsp vinegar

juice of ½ lemon

¼ cup warm water

¼ tsp salt

¼ tsp chili powder

¼ tsp cumin

1 garlic clove

¼ tsp olive oil

_____

Tahina is made from sesame seed paste, and is one of the most popular Egyptian dips. If the prepared paste is not available, you can easily make it. Preheat the oven to 180°C. Place 200g/1 cup of seeds in a pan, and toast in the oven until they just begin to change color, but don't let the seeds get brown. When ready, put the sesame seeds in a blender, then add 1 tsp corn oil and mix until it becomes thick and creamy.

Baba Ghanoug Dip

Eggplant Dip

Serves: 2 - 4 | Preparation time: 10 minutes
            Baking time: 40 minutes for the eggplant

1. Preheat oven to 260° C.
2. Wash the eggplants and dry well, leaving the skin on.
3. Poke the eggplants all over with a fork; then with a brush, spread olive oil on them to help release the juices while cooking.
4. Put the eggplants and onions in a pan and bake in oven about 30 minutes, until each side darkens and becomes tender.
5. Remove from oven and allow to cool.
6. Peel and mash the baked eggplants and onions in a separate bowl.
7. Add lemon juice to the mashed eggplants to help preserve the color.
8. Mince the garlic, and add it to the bowl.
9. Add *tahina* (sesame paste), vinegar, chili, and salt.
10. Blend all ingredients by hand to obtain a chunky texture.
11. Transfer to a serving plate and add ¼ tsp olive oil, then sprinkle fresh chopped parsley on top.

Best served cold with Egyptian *baladi* (pita) bread.

2 large eggplants (aubergine; about 1kg / 2 lbs)

1 tsp olive oil

2 medium onions (about 200g), chopped

juice of 2 small lemons (about 100g)

1 garlic clove

2 tbsp *tahina* (sesame paste)

¼ tsp vinegar

¼ tsp chili powder

¼ tsp salt

½ tsp chopped parsley

_____

Baba ghanoug is one of Egypt's most popular dips. It is supposed to be chunky, so make sure it is not too smooth when blended. Eggplant is known in Egypt as bitingan roumi, which refers to its foreign origins in Turkey.

Yogurt, Cucumber, and Mint Dip

Serves: 2 - 4 | Preparation time: 10 minutes

1. Mix yogurt and salt with chopped garlic in a blender, and transfer to a bowl.
2. Peel and grate the cucumber. Drain the water from the cucumber, and add to the yogurt and garlic mix.
3. Transfer to serving plate and garnish with dried mint.

Best served with the stuffed vine leaves known as *mahshi waraq enab* (see p.43), or with toasted bread cut into 1-inch cubes.

1 liter / 4 cups yogurt

¼ tsp salt

1 garlic clove, chopped fine

1 small cucumber (about 75g)

¼ tsp dried mint

This is best eaten fresh on the same day it is prepared. It is a perfect choice of appetizer or mezza, complementing any Egyptian meal.

Oriental Salad

Serves: 2 - 4 | Preparation time: 10 minutes

1. Wash the raw vegetables thoroughly. Cut or grate the tomatoes, cucumbers, and onion evenly into thin, long slices, and mix together in a bowl. Shred the lettuce and watercress, and add.

Dressing
2. Whisk together the lemon juice, vinegar, oil, salt, and cumin.
3. Add to the vegetables and greens, and toss well.

Serve immediately.

3 large tomatoes (about 600g)

2 small cucumbers (about 150g)

1 medium onion (about 250g)

½ head small lettuce (about 150g)

1 bunch watercress (about 100g)

juice of ½ lemon

1 tbsp vinegar

1 tsp oil

¼ tsp salt

½ tsp cumin

Oriental salad, known as salata baladi, is a light, ready-to-eat dish in every Egyptian home. It is usually served with every meal.

Bessara

Fava and Coriander Dip

Serves: 2 - 4 | Preparation time: 15 minutes
Cooking time: 30 minutes

1. Wash the dried white beans very well. Combine the beans, 3 garlic cloves, coriander, dill, parsley, black pepper, salt, mint powder, chili powder, and 3¼ cups water in a saucepan.
Bring to a boil, and cook for 30 minutes. Transfer the mixture to a blender and blend until well combined, and dark green in color.
2. Return the mixture to the pan, bring to a boil, lower the heat, and cook for 15 minutes.
3. Remove from heat and add salt and chili powder.
4. In a pan, fry the remaining garlic in a little corn oil until it changes color, and then add dried coriander and cook on low heat until it becomes golden brown. Add to the bean mixture and you will hear "tshhhh." This is known as *tasha* in Arabic.
5. Transfer to a serving plate.
6. Slice the onion thinly, and fry it with 2 tbsp corn oil in another pan until the slices turn deep brown and caramelize. Drain the oil from the onions, and sprinkle over the *bessara*.

Best served at room temperature.

700g / 3 cups dried white (fava) beans
6 garlic cloves, chopped
250ml / 1 cup coriander leaves
1 tbsp chopped dill
250ml / 1 cup parsley leaves
¼ tsp black pepper
1 tsp salt
½ tsp dried mint powder
¼ tsp chili powder
2 tbsp corn oil
1 tsp dried coriander
500g / 1 lb onions (about 4)

Bessara is one of the main dishes in Egyptian homes, and especially popular in Christian homes, as it is a very nourishing dish on fasting days.

Abou El Sid Lentils

Serves: 2 - 4 | Preparation time: 10 minutes
Cooking time: 30 minutes

1. Rinse the lentils several times.
2. Boil 2 cups of water. Add the lentils, 1 garlic clove, minced onions, 1 grated carrot, 1 chopped tomato, and shredded potatoes and boil for 20 minutes, until the lentils and vegetables are cooked but still firm. Do not overcook to the point of mushiness.
3. Drain the leftover water with a sieve.
4. Blend the lentils and vegetables in a blender, then return to the pan and heat on low.
5. In another pan, put the remaining grated carrot with the remaining tomato, chopped into tiny pieces, and mix with 1 tbsp butter on low heat with ¼ cup of water for 5 minutes.
   Combine both mixtures together in one pan, and add salt and chili.
6. In a different pan, heat the remaining chopped garlic clove in corn oil, stirring until it turns golden brown. Then add 1 tsp chopped coriander leaves, and stir with the garlic. When ready, toss on hot lentil mix, and you will hear "tshhhh." This sound is known as *tasha* in Arabic.
7. Cool, refrigerate, and serve.

Best served cold with Egyptian *baladi* (pita) bread.

225g / 1 cup yellow lentils

2 large garlic cloves, chopped

2 medium onions (about 250g)

2 carrots (about 150g), grated

2 large tomatoes (about 400g)

1 medium potato (about 100g)

1 tbsp butter

1 tsp salt

¼ tsp chili powder

3 tbsp corn oil

1 tsp chopped coriander leaves

Yellow lentils are very popular in Egyptian cuisine. This dish is inexpensive, filling, nutritious, and easy to make. It is sometimes used as a meat substitute in the Christian fasting menu.

Kishk with Yogurt

Serves: 2 - 4 | Preparation time: 30 minutes
Cooking time: 15 minutes

1. Combine milk with flour, chicken stock or broth.
2. Mix well in blender. Cover and let stand for 30 minutes.
3. Heat 2 tbsp oil in a pan with 1 tbsp grated onion and white pepper. Cook, stirring, until the mixture browns.
4. Add chicken soup, and bring to a boil.
5. Lower the heat, and slowly whisk in the yogurt, stirring thoroughly until it is smooth and creamy. Add 1 tbsp of ghee, and keep mixing.
6. Add lemon juice to the mixture and let cool. Transfer to a serving dish.
7. Slice the onion thinly, and fry in a pan with a little more ghee until it turns a deep golden brown.
8. Sprinkle the caramelized onions over the *kishk*.

Best served at room temperature with Egyptian *baladi* (pita) bread.

¼ cup milk

2 tbsp flour

2 chicken stock cubes in 3
     cups of water, or 3 cups
     salted chicken stock

500ml / 2 cups yogurt

2 tbsp corn oil

1 onion (about 125g) plus 1
     tbsp grated onion

¼ tsp white pepper

1 tbsp ghee or clarified butter

juice of 2 lemons

Kishk can be made with plain chicken broth or with yogurt added, but the two have completely different tastes. Its appeal lies in the fact that the dish is abundant in umami, described as savory deliciousness, found in foods like meats, broth, some vegetables, and fermented products.

Spicy Cheese Dip

Serves: 2 - 4 | Preparation time: 10 minutes

1. Dice the tomatoes into small 2 cm x 2 cm / 1 in x 1 in pieces.
2. Beat the feta cheese, and mix in the chili and corn oil, combining until the mixture is smooth. Add the tomatoes.
3. Transfer to a serving plate, sprinkle chopped parsley on top, and garnish with olive oil.

Best served cold, with Egyptian *baladi* (pita) bread.

2 tomatoes (about 250g)

500g / 1 lb feta cheese (the creamy feta sold in containers works better for this recipe than the drier types)

¼ tsp chili powder

1 tbsp corn oil

2 tbsp parsley

1 tsp olive oil

Spicy cheese dip is one of Egypt's most famous dips. It can be served for breakfast or as a mezza or appetizer for other meals.

Stuffed Vine Leaves

Serves: 2 - 4 | Preparation time: 30 minutes

Preparing the stuffing

1. Put ground meat in a bowl and add the grated onions, minced garlic, salt, chili, and white pepper.
2. Wash the rice well, drain, and add it uncooked to the bowl with the meat.
3. Peel 3 tomatoes and chop them fine. Add 1 grated carrot and the tomato sauce.
4. Finely chop the fresh dill, parsley, coriander, and mint, and further mince in a blender or food processor. Add the olive oil and combine well.

Preparing the vine leaves

5. If fresh vine leaves are used, rinse them well and parboil in salted water for 2 minutes. If frozen, just rinse. If a vine leaf is large, you can cut it into 2 pieces to keep them all a uniform size. Remove the center stalks of the leaves with a sharp knife.
6. Arrange the stalks neatly in the bottom of a pot.
7. Cut the remaining carrot and tomato into round slices.
8. Arrange carrots, tomato, and mint in layers over the stalks.
9. On a flat surface, place the inner veined sides of the leaves facing up and the shiny outer sides facing down.
10. Stuff each vine leaf with 1 tsp of the stuffing mix; roll tightly in a pencil shape, folding the right and left sides in neatly as you roll.
11. Arrange the stuffed vine leaves in the pot in a circular shape, in layers, on top of the stalks. Allow enough space in the pot for the vine leaves to expand.
12. Mix the meat broth or vegetable broth with ¾ cup water. Bring it to a boil, pour over the vine leaves, cover, and simmer on low to moderate heat for 30 minutes.
13. Season with olive oil and lemon juice.
14. Transfer to a serving plate.
15. Garnish with dried mint, and serve warm.

Best served with Yogurt and Mint Dip.

400g / 1 lb ground beef and lamb combined

2 tbsp grated onions

4 garlic cloves, minced finely

1 tsp salt

¼ tsp chili powder

1 tsp white pepper

200g / 1 cup rice

4 large tomatoes (about 800g)

2 carrots

1 tbsp tomato sauce

2 bunches fresh dill (about 50g)

1 bunch parsley (about 50g)

2 bunches fresh coriander (cilantro, about 100g)

2 bunches fresh mint (about 100g)

2 tbsp olive oil

500g / 1 lb vine leaves

1 meat or vegetable broth cube

juice of 4 small lemons (about 200g)

½ tsp dried mint

Stuffed vine leaves are one of the most popular appetizers in Egypt and the Middle East.

Fried Eggplant

with Garlic and Vinegar

Serves: 2 - 4 | Preparation time: 30 minutes

1. Slice eggplants into rounds, about ½cm / ¼ inch thick.
2. Heat the corn oil in a pan, and fry the eggplant slices until they turn brown.
3. Remove the eggplant slices from the oil with a slotted spoon, and drain on paper towels. Place on a serving plate. Slice the tomatoes into rounds and add them to the serving plate.
4. In a bowl, combine the olive oil, mustard, vinegar, lemon, garlic, cumin, salt, chili, and water.
5. Add to the eggplant and tomatoes, and let it sit for 10 minutes so the flavors can combine before serving.
6. Garnish with finely chopped fresh parsley.

Best served cold with Egyptian *baladi* (pita) bread.

2 large eggplants (about 1kg / 2 lbs)

400ml / 1½ cups corn oil

4 large tomatoes (about 800g)

1 tsp olive oil

1 tsp mustard

1 tbsp vinegar

juice of ½ lemon

4 garlic cloves, pressed or very finely chopped

½ tsp cumin

¼ tsp salt

¼ tsp chili powder

2 tbsp water

1 bunch parsley

This appetizer is part of the Egyptian family of pickled vegetables.

Oriental Fuul

Fava Beans with Bell Peppers and Onions

Serves: 2 - 4 | Preparation time: 15 minutes

1. Simmer the beans slowly in water for 10 minutes in a covered pan over medium-low heat.
2. Finely chop the onions and green bell peppers into small squares.
3. Heat the butter with the sunflower oil in a pan, and add the vegetables. Sauté them until they begin to brown. Add the beans to this mix, and add the cumin, salt, chili, and lemon juice.
4. Transfer to a serving bowl. Add tomato and finely chopped fresh parsley on top. Drizzle with olive oil.

Best served with small pieces of *baladi* bread.

500ml / 2 cups canned fava beans
2 medium onions (about 250g)
2 green bell peppers
1 tbsp butter
2 tbsp sunflower oil
½ tsp cumin
¼ tsp salt
⅛ tsp chili powder
juice of ½ lemon
small amount of chopped parsley
1 tomato (about 200g)
1 tsp olive oil

Fuul is stewed fava beans, known in Arabic as fuul meddamis, the national Egyptian breakfast.

Fuul with Tahina

Fava Beans with Tahina Sauce

Serves: 2 - 4 | Preparation time: 15 minutes

1. Simmer the beans slowly for 5 minutes in a covered pan over medium heat. Purée the beans in a bender.
2. Heat the butter in a pan. Add the puréed beans, and stir in the cumin, salt, and chili.
3. Transfer to a serving bowl, and add the *tahina* and finely chopped fresh parsley on top. Drizzle with olive oil.

Best served hot with small pieces of *baladi* bread.

500ml / 2 cups canned fava beans
1 tbsp butter
½ tsp cumin
¼ tsp salt
⅛ tsp chili
4 tbsp *tahina*
small amount of chopped parsley
1 tsp olive oil

Fuul is stewed fava beans, known in Arabic as fuul meddamis, the national Egyptian breakfast. Tahina is made from sesame seed paste, one of the most popular Egyptian dips. It complements fuul and many other Egyptian plates and sandwiches.

Taameya

Falafel

Serves: 2 - 4 | Preparation time: 3–12 hours for soaking the dried garbanzo beans
Cooking time: 30 minutes

1. If using dried white garbanzo beans, soak in cold water a minimum of 3 hours, or overnight; if using canned chickpeas or white broad beans, soak for 30 minutes.
2. In a food processor fitted with the steel blade, grind the spring onions, cilantro, garlic, onions, and green chili peppers, until the mixture is finely chopped. Or chop all ingredients together with a large knife.
3. Put in a bowl and add the garbanzo beans, parsley, and salt.
4. Mix well, mashing the garbanzo beans into the mixture.
5. Using a large spoon, scoop out portions of the mixture and form into patties about 2 inches in diameter.
6. Dip both sides of the patties in sesame seeds.
7. Deep-fry for 5 minutes in corn oil, turning the patties as they become golden brown in color. Remove the patties with a slotted spoon, and drain on paper towels before serving.

500 g / 2 cups dried white garbanzo beans (chickpeas) or canned chickpeas or white broad beans

1 bunch spring onions (scallions)

2 bunches cilantro (coriander)

6 cloves garlic

2 large onions (about 250g)

100g / 2 green chili peppers

1 bunch parsley, chopped fine

1 tsp salt

1 tbsp sesame seeds

12 tbsp corn oil

Taameya is known as falafel in other parts of the Middle East, where it is made with chickpeas. In Egypt, it is made with fava beans. Suitable for vegetarians, it is one of the most classic Egyptian fast foods, and is eaten at breakfast and throughout the day. Taameya is best served hot or at room temperature, slipped into halves of the Egyptian round loaves known as baladi bread, and garnished with tahina and salad.

Fried Eggs with Pastrami

Serves: 2 - 4 | Preparation time: 7 minutes

1. Heat the corn oil and the butter in a pan.
2. Crack the eggs and drop into the heated pan, leaving the sunny side up. Cook for 1 minute.
3. Cut the pastrami slices in rectangular pieces, and spread evenly around on the white part of the egg. Cook for 5 minutes.
4. Transfer to a plate, and sprinkle black pepper on top.

Serve immediately with Egyptian *baladi* bread

1 tbsp corn oil

1 tbsp butter

4 eggs

125g / ¼ lb pastrami

¼ tsp black pepper

Fried eggs with pastrami is a famous Egyptian breakfast dish. Many Egyptians cook it at home on weekends.

Lamb Kofta or Tarb

Serves: 2 - 4 | Preparation time: 30 minutes

1. Preheat the grill or oven broiler.
2. Mix meat and fat with onion, salt, white pepper, mixed spices, and corn oil.
3. Shape the meat into cylindrical pieces 4cm (1½ inches) wide by 7cm (about 3 inches) long.
4. Brush oil on the *kofta* to keep them from sticking on the grill while cooking.
5. Grill until cooked according to your taste.

Best served with Egyptian *baladi* bread (pita) and *tahina* sauce.

500g / 1 lb ground lamb

½ tsp minced lamb fat

1 onion (about 250g), grated

½ tsp salt

¼ tsp white pepper

½ tsp mixed spices

1 tbsp corn oil

_____

This recipe is the Egyptian Abou El Sid way of grilling minced meat.

Spicy Oriental Sausage

Serves: 2 - 4 | Preparation time: 30 minutes

1. Heat a pan with oil, and add to it round slices of onions and minced garlic. Sauté until golden brown.
2. Add the sausage and continue cooking for 5 minutes.
3. Peel the tomatoes, and purée them in a blender with ½ cup water and tomato paste.
4. Strain the tomato juice through a sieve, and pour it over the sausage mixture. Cook over medium heat for 15 minutes.
5. Add the salt and the chili.
6. When almost cooked, add the thinly sliced green pepper to the sausage mix and keep stirring for 2 more minutes.
7. Garnish with finely chopped parsley and serve.

Best served hot with Egyptian *baladi* bread (pita), or *shami* bread, plain or toasted.

2 tbsp corn oil

2 medium onions (about 250g)

4 garlic cloves, minced

500g / 1 lb oriental sausage

1 large tomato (about 200g)

1 tbsp tomato paste

¼ tsp salt

¼ tsp chili powder

1 green pepper (about 100g), thinly sliced

1 parsley sprig

Oriental sausages can be purchased from butchers and meat counters, salted and ready to cook.

Kobeba

Fried Cracked Wheat and Lamb Meatballs

Serves: 2 - 4 | Preparation time: 30 minutes

1. Soak the cracked wheat in water for 15 minutes.
2. Mix all ingredients, except the pine nuts, mint, and corn oil using a food processor, until the mixture is well combined.
3. Combine the pine nuts and mint in a separate bowl.
4. Roll the meat mixture into balls with the palms of the hands.
5. Press the pine nuts into the center of the balls, and close up the hole.
6. Heat the corn oil in a pan over a low flame, and fry the *kobeba* for about 10 minutes until they brown.

Best served hot with Baba Ghanoug dip.

225g / 1 cup cracked wheat

250ml / 1 cup corn oil

250g / ½ lb ground lamb

1 tsp salt

¼ tsp pepper

¼ tsp ground cinnamon

¼ tsp mixed spices

1 red bell pepper (about 50g), chopped finely

1 tbsp pine nuts

1 tsp dried mint

Kobeba is also known as kibbeh in other areas of the Middle East.

Chicken Livers Alexandrian Style

Serves: 2 - 4 | Preparation time: 30 minutes

1. Wash the chicken livers well with water, and pat dry.
2. Chop the livers and the onions into squares 3cm x 3cm (about 1¼ inch x 1¼ inch).
3. Heat the corn oil in a pan, and fry the chicken livers for 10 minutes.
4. Remove the livers from the pan and keep warm. Add the butter, garlic, red chili pepper, salt, and black pepper to the onions in the pan. Sauté until the garlic and onions turn golden brown.
5. Transfer to a serving plate, add the chicken livers to it, and season with lemon juice.

Serve with Egyptian *baladi* bread (pita).

500g / 1 lb chicken livers

250g / ½ lb onions

4 tbsp corn oil

½ tbsp butter

2 garlic cloves, finely chopped

2 red chili peppers (about ½g), sliced

¼ tsp salt

¼ tsp black pepper

juice of ½ lemon (about 25g)

_____

Although the origins of this dish lie in the city of Alexandria, it is popular all over Egypt.

Grilled Quail

Serves: 2 - 4 | Preparation time: 45 minutes

Preparing the quail
1. Remove both wings.
2. Using scissors, remove both legs and joints.
3. Remove the head, cutting close to the body.
4. Remove the skin and feathers.
5. Remove the tail, cutting close to the body.
6. Remove the intestines, lungs, and heart.
7. Split the quails in half, and flatten, using a meat mallet.
8. Rinse with warm water.

Marinade
9. Peel the onions and the tomatoes, purée them in a blender, then strain the liquid into a bowl.
10. Add the corn oil, salt, white pepper, mixed spices, and mustard, and the quail to the liquid in the bowl.
11. Marinate for 10 minutes.
12. Remove the quail from the marinade, brush with oil, and grill until browned.
13. After grilling, heat the butter in a pan over medium heat, and sauté the quail for a short time. Remove, add lemon juice, and serve with *tahina*.

4 quail

2 onions (about 250g / ½ lb)

2 tomatoes (about 250g / ½ lb)

2 tbsp corn oil

1 tsp salt

¼ tsp white pepper

½ tsp mixed spices

1 tsp mustard

1½ tsp butter

juice of 2 lemons (about 100g)

Grilled quail are a favorite in every Egyptian home. It can seem intimidating to make, but once the birds have been cleaned and dressed, it is easy and fast.

Mini Veal Kebab Brochette

Serves: 2 - 4 | Preparation time: 45 minutes

1. Cut the veal kebab in cubes, 4cm x 4cm (1½ inches x 1½ inches).
2. Cut 2 of the onions and both of the green peppers into squares 3cm x 3cm (1¼ inches x 1¼ inches).

Marinade
3. Peel the remaining onion and the tomatoes. Purée them in a blender, then strain the liquid into a bowl.
4. Add the corn oil, salt, white pepper, mixed spices, mustard, and veal.
5. Marinate for 10 minutes.

Preparing the kebabs
6. Thread the onions, green peppers, and veal onto the skewers, in that order.
7. Brush veal cubes with oil, and grill until they turn gold. Sauté them in warm butter and the marinade mix.

Best served with Egyptian *baladi* bread (pita) and *tahina*.

500g / 1 lb veal kebab

3 onions (about 300g / ½ lb)

2 green peppers

2 tomatoes (about 250g / ½ lb)

2 tbsp corn oil

1 tsp salt

¼ tsp white pepper

½ tsp mixed spices

1 tsp mustard

6 wooden or metal skewers

_____

Only Abou El Sid prepares its Mini Veal Kebab Brochette in this special way.

Stuffed Mombar Sausage

Serves: 2 - 4 | Preparation time: 1 hour, 15 minutes

1. Chop the coriander, parsley, and dill.
2. Finely chop or grind the onions and garlic in a food processor.
3. Heat onions and garlic in a deep pan with oil until they brown.
4. Wash the rice well, and add to the onions and garlic.
5. Add the tomato paste and ½ cup of water and stir for 5 minutes.
6. Add the chili, pepper, coriander, parsley, dill, and 1½ tsp salt.
7. Mix well, and allow to cool.
8. Using a long, thin wooden spoon handle, turn the chitterlings inside out.
9. Roll them in a mixture of vinegar, flour, and 1½ tsp salt.
10. Turn inside out again, and rinse with water.
11. Stuff the rice mixture into the chitterlings, taking care not to over-stuff, as the rice will expand as it cooks.
12. Tie both ends with string.
13. Peel the tomatoes, extract the juice, and put the juice into a deep pan.
14. Add the bay leaves, cardamom pods, and sausages, and boil for 20 minutes on high.
15. Remove the string from the sausages, and fry them in oil for 5 minutes.
16. Cut the sausages into 2cm / ¾-inch pieces, and serve.

1kg / 2 lbs beef chitterlings or sausage casings

2 bunches coriander (cilantro)

1 bunch parsley

1 bunch dill

5 medium onions (about 500g / 1 lb)

10 garlic cloves (about 100g / 3 ounces)

500ml / 2 cups corn oil

500g / 2½ cups rice

2 tbsp tomato paste

1 tsp chili powder

1 tbsp salt

¼ tsp black pepper

1 tbsp vinegar

1 tbsp flour

8 medium tomatoes

4 bay leaves

4 cardamom pods

This dish may not be easy to make for the first time, but it is done in every Egyptian home.

Veal Liver Alexandrian Style

Serves: 2 - 4 | Preparation time: 25 minutes

1. Wash the veal liver well with water, and pat dry.
2. Chop the liver and the onions into squares 3cm x 3cm (about 1¼ inch x 1¼ inch).
3. Heat the corn oil in a pan, and fry the liver for 5 minutes.
4. Remove the liver from the pan and keep warm. Add the butter, onions, garlic, green chili peppers, salt, and black pepper to the pan. Sauté until the garlic and onions turn golden brown.
5. Transfer to a serving plate, add the liver to it, and season with lemon juice.

Serve with Egyptian *baladi* bread (pita).

500g / 1 lb veal liver

250g / ½ lb onions

4 tbsp corn oil

½ tbsp butter

2 garlic cloves, finely chopped

2 green chili peppers (about ½ g), sliced

¼ tsp salt

¼ tsp black pepper

juice of ½ lemon (about 25g)

_____

Although the origins of this dish lie in the city of Alexandria, it is popular all over Egypt.

Mahshi

Serves: 2 - 4 | Preparation time: 1 hour, 15 minutes

Stuffing

1. Put ground beef in a bowl and add the grated onions, minced garlic, salt, chili powder, and white pepper.
2. Wash the rice well, drain, and add to the bowl.
3. Finely chop the dill, parsley, coriander, and mint, setting aside the mint stalks. Add the olive oil, add the seasonings to the meat mixture, and combine thoroughly.
4. Peel and chop the 3 tomatoes coarsely. Combine the tomatoes, carrot rounds, and tomato sauce.

Preparing the vegetables

5. Core the eggplants, zucchini, peppers, and tomatoes, removing all stems and seeds.
6. Stuff the vegetables fairly loosely with the mixture, taking care to leave space for the filling to expand while cooking.
7. Chop up the mint stalks with a sharp knife. Arrange them over the bottom of a deep pot. On top of them, arrange the stuffed vegetables neatly in layers. Allow space in the pot for the vegetables to expand a bit.
8. Dissolve the cube of vegetable or beef broth in 2 cups of water.
9. Add the broth and the tomato paste to the pot.
10. Bring it to boil, then cover, and cook over moderate heat for 30 minutes.
11. Season with olive oil.
12. Transfer the stuffed vegetables to a serving plate.
13. Serve warm, garnished with dried or chopped fresh mint.

Mahshi is the Arabic name for stuffed vegetables. It is a colorful, fresh dish, with the same stuffing as vine leaves, but it looks and tastes different. It is a popular main course in Egypt and the Middle East.

500g / 1 lb ground beef or veal
2 tbsp grated onions
4 garlic cloves, minced
1 tsp salt
¼ tsp chili powder
1 tsp white pepper
225g / 1 cup rice
2 bunches fresh dill (about 50g / 2 oz)
1 bunch fresh parsley (about 50g / 2 oz)
2 bunches fresh coriander (cilantro, about 100g / 4 oz)
2 bunches fresh mint (about 100g / 4 oz)
2 tbsp olive oil
3 large tomatoes (about 600g / 1½ lb)
1 carrot, cut into rounds
1 tbsp tomato sauce
5 medium white eggplant (about 250g / ½ lb)
5 medium purple eggplant (about 250g / ½ lb)
5 medium zucchini (about 250g / ½ lb)
6 medium green sweet bell peppers (about 250g / ½ lb)
4 medium tomatoes (about 250g / ½ lb)
1 cube vegetable or beef broth
1 tbsp tomato paste
chopped mint, fresh or dried

main courses

Mesakaa

Eggplant with minced meat

Serves: 2 - 4 | Preparation time: 30 minutes

Preparing the eggplant
1. Preheat oven to 160°C / 320°F.
2. Wash the eggplant and slice into rounds.
3. Heat the corn oil in a pan, and fry the eggplant and red chili pepper over medium heat until the eggplant turns golden brown.
4. Lift the eggplant slices and chilis from the oil and place them on paper towels to drain.

Preparing the meat
5. In a pan, warm the same oil in which the eggplant was fried over medium heat, and add minced onions, bay leaves, and garlic. Stir until they become yellow.
6. Add the meat, salt, and pepper and stir for about 15 minutes, until the meat turns brown.
7. Add the tomato paste and ¼ cup of water and keep mixing until all is well combined.
8. Remove the bay leaves from the meat.
9. In a *lagin*, layer the meat, then the fried eggplant, chili pepper, another layer of meat, eggplant, and chili pepper.
10. Decoratively garnish the eggplant with thin rounds of tomato and green pepper. Add meat sauce on top.
11. Heat in the oven for 10 minutes before serving.

Serve at room temperature with Egyptian *baladi* bread.

2 large eggplants (aubergine, about 500g / 1 lb)

250ml / 1 cup corn oil

2 large red chili peppers (about 250g / ½ lb)

2 large onions (about 250g / ½ lb)

5 garlic cloves, crushed

250g / ½ lb ground meat (beef or veal)

1 tsp salt

¼ tsp white pepper

2 tbsp tomato paste

Rounds of tomato and green pepper for garnish

2 bay leaves

———————————————

Eggplant is known in Egypt as bitingan roumi, which alludes to its foreign origins in Turkey.

Spinach and Veal Tagin

Serves: 2 - 4 | Preparation time: 40 minutes

1. Preheat oven to 100° C / 200°F.
2. Boil the chickpeas for 20 minutes.
3. Drain, and put the chickpeas aside to use later to garnish the plate.

Preparing the meat

4. Put the meat, celery, carrot, cardamom pods, white pepper, and salt to boil in 2½ cups water on low heat for 30 minutes. For extra seasoning add a beef stock cube.
5. Remove the meat, put aside, and reserve the meat stock for the spinach preparation.

Preparing the spinach

6. Heat the corn oil in a pan over medium heat.
7. Add the minced onion, and sauté until it browns.
8. Cut the spinach in long slices, and add to the pan.
9. Add the meat stock to the spinach, and cook over medium heat, stirring.
10. Add 3/4 of the chickpeas to the mix.
11. Peel and dice the tomato, and add to the spinach.

Preparing the tasha

12. In another pan, cook the butter and crushed garlic in 1 tsp corn oil, stirring, until it turns golden brown. Add 1 tsp chopped coriander leaves and stir. When you toss it on the spinach at the very end, you will hear "tshhhh." This is known as *tasha* in Arabic.
13. Place the spinach in a *tagin*, then add the meat on top. Garnish with the remaining chickpeas.
14. Heat in the oven for 5 minutes before serving. Serve with white rice.

2 tbsp canned chickpeas

800g / 1¾ lb veal

1 stalk celery

1 carrot (about 75g / 2½ oz)

3 cardamom pods

¼ tsp white pepper

¼ tsp salt

1 beef stock cube

2 tbsp corn oil

2 medium onions (about 250g / ½ lb), minced

1kg / 2 lbs fresh spinach

1 tomato (about 200g / 7 oz)

1 tsp butter

4 garlic cloves, crushed

1 tsp cilantro (coriander) leaves, finely chopped

A tagin is an Arabic earthenware pot made of heavy clay in which the dish is cooked.

Artichoke and Veal Tagin

Serves: 2 - 4 | Preparation time: 45 minutes

Preheat the oven to 160°C / 320°F.

Preparing the meat

1. Cut veal into cubes sized 4cm x 4cm (1½ inches x 1½ inches).
2. Boil the meat, celery, 1½ carrots, cardamom pods, white pepper, and salt for 30 minutes. For extra seasoning, add beef stock cubes.
3. Drain the meat with a sieve and set it aside. Keep the meat broth to be used later with the artichokes.

Preparing the artichoke hearts

4. Cut the artichokes in half.
5. Chop the onions into thin slices.
6. Chop the carrots into rounds.
7. Heat the oil and butter in a pan, and add the onions and the remaining carrots. Stir until quite tender.
8. Add the flour very slowly and stir continuously to avoid lumps.
9. Add the meat stock and the bay leaves, and boil for 5 minutes.
10. Add the artichokes and lemon juice, and simmer until cooked, about 5 minutes.

11. Put the meat and the artichokes into a *tagin*. Heat in the oven for 5 minutes before serving.

Serve with white rice.

500g / 1 lb veal

1 bunch celery

3 medium-sized carrots (about ½ kg)

3 cardamom pods

¼ tsp white pepper

¼ tsp salt

12 canned artichoke hearts (about 800g / 1¾ lb)

2 large onions (about 250g / ½ lb)

1 tbsp flour

2 beef stock cubes

2 bay leaves

1 tbsp corn oil

1 tbsp butter

2 lemons (about 100g / 3½ oz) if using canned artichoke; 4 lemons if using fresh artichoke

---

This is a unique Egyptian dish as it is cooked with white sauce, which is unusual in Egyptian cuisine. If using fresh artichokes, 2 kilograms (4½ lbs) replaces the 12 canned artichoke hearts. Squeeze the juice of 4 lemons over the fresh artichokes to preserve their color.

Veal Tagin with Fireek

Serves: 2 - 4 | Preparation time: 60 minutes

1. Preheat the oven to 160°C / 320°F.
2. Wash the *fireek* very well and soak in water for 30 minutes.

Preparing the meat
3. Cut the meat into cubes 4cm x 4cm (1½ inches x 1½ inches).
4. Boil the meat, celery, cardamom pods, white pepper, and salt for 30 minutes. For extra seasoning, add the beef stock cube.
5. Drain the meat with a sieve and set it aside. Keep the meat stock to use later with the *fireek*.
6. Heat the corn oil in a pan, then fry the meat over low heat.

Preparing the *fireek*
7. Heat the oil and butter in a deep pan.
8. Add the onions and stir until they turn golden brown.
9. Add the *fireek*, 3 cups of meat stock, salt, and white pepper, and simmer for 15 minutes on low heat, until all the liquid is absorbed.

10. Layer *fireek*, then meat, and then *fireek* again in a *tagin*. Heat in the oven for 5 minutes before serving.

500g / 1 lb boneless veal

1 bunch celery, chopped

3 cardamom pods

½ tsp white pepper

½ tsp salt

1 beef stock cube

1 tbsp corn oil

2 tbsp butter

2 large onions (about 250g / ½ lb), finely chopped

500g / 1 lb dried green wheat (*fireek*)

Fireek is a famous dish in Egypt, but is fairly uncommon outside the Middle East. It is made from green wheat; the seeds are collected during the harvest, when they are still soft, and sun-dried. Rice or shaareya can be used instead, but the fireek has a uniquely crunchy texture.

Okra and Veal Tagin

Serves: 2 - 4 | Preparation time: 40 minutes

Preheat the oven to 100°C / 212°F.

Preparing the meat

1: Dust the meat with flour. Fry in oil until it turns dark golden brown.
2. Boil 4 cups of water in a pot, and then add the fried veal and cook for 30 minutes. Add ½ tsp salt, ½ tsp pepper, and, for extra seasoning, a beef stock cube.
3. Drain the meat with a sieve, and set it aside.

Preparing the okra

4. Grate the onions and heat in a pan with corn oil, stirring until they turn golden brown.
5. Peel the tomato and grate it and the carrot. Add to the pan.
6. Add the tomato paste, cardamom pods, ½ tsp salt, and ½ tsp pepper to the pan.
7. Add the okra, and sauté until cooked.
8. In another pan, heat the crushed garlic with the corn oil, stirring until it turns golden brown. Then add the coriander leaves, and stir until it shrivels up with the garlic.
9. Add this mixture to the okra, and you will hear "tshhhh." This is known as *tasha* in Arabic.
10. Place in a *tagin*, putting the okra on the bottom and the meat on top. Heat in the oven for 10 minutes.

Serve with white rice.

800g / 1¾ lb boneless veal

2 tbsp flour

180ml / ¾ cup corn oil

1 tsp salt

1 tsp white pepper

1 beef stock cube

2 medium-sized onions (about 250g / ½ lb)

1 tomato (about 200g / 7 oz)

2 tbsp tomato paste

1 carrot (about 75g / 2½ oz)

1kg / 2 lb okra

3 cardamom pods

4 cloves garlic, crushed

1 tbsp coriander (cilantro), finely chopped

_____

Okra is known in different countries as okro, lady's fingers, and bamya. It is a popular dish in Egyptian cuisine.

Veal and Orzo Tagin

Serves: 2 – 4 | Preparation time: 1 hour 20 minutes

1. Preheat the oven to 100°C / 200°F.

Preparing the veal

2. Dust the meat with flour.
3. Fry in oil until it turns dark golden brown.
4. Boil 4 cups water in a pot, and simmer the veal in it for 30 minutes.
5. Add 1 tsp salt and 1 tsp pepper; for extra seasoning, add a beef stock cube.
6. Remove the meat and set aside.

Preparing the pasta

7. Fry the orzo in oil, adding ½ tsp salt, ¼ tsp pepper, and cinnamon. Cook until it turns golden brown. Remove the orzo from the oil using a slotted spoon, and drain.
8. Cook the orzo in 2 cups of water with 2 beef stock cubes for 20 minutes.

Preparing the brown meat sauce

9. In another pan, sauté the chopped onions in the oil, stirring, until it turns dark brown. Then add the cardamom pods, chopped celery, grated carrot, peeled and grated tomato, salt, pepper, and 2½ cups water, and stir. Add flour and stir until sauce reaches the desired thickness. Cover and cook for 15 minutes.
10. Place the orzo in a *tagin*, then add the meat on top. Garnish with the brown sauce. Heat in the oven for 10 minutes, and serve.

800g / 1¾ lb boneless veal

2 tbsp flour

180ml / ¾ cup corn oil

1½ tsp salt

1¼ tsp white pepper

3 beef stock cubes

500g / 2 cups orzo pasta

¼ tsp ground cinnamon

1 large onion (about 100g / 3½ oz)

3 cardamom pods

1 bunch celery

1 carrot (about 75g / 2½ oz), grated

1 tomato (about 200g / 7 oz), peeled and chopped fine.

The Arabic name of the pasta in this dish, lisan 'asfour, comes from its shape. It translates literally as 'bird's tongue.'

Veal and Pearl Onion Tagin

Serves: 2 – 4 | Preparation time: 40 minutes

Preheat oven to 160°C / 320°F.

Preparing the veal
1. Dust the meat with flour. Fry in oil until it turns dark golden brown.
2. Boil 4 cups of water in a pot, and add the veal and cook for 30 minutes. Add ½ tsp salt, ½ tsp pepper and, for extra seasoning, the beef stock cube.
3. Drain the meat with a sieve, and set it aside.

Preparing the brown sauce
4. In another pan, heat the chopped onions in the same corn oil in which the meat was fried, stirring until they turn dark brown.
5. Add the cardamom pods, celery, ½ tsp salt, ½ tsp pepper, grated carrot, tomato, meat broth, cinnamon, and 1½ cups water and mix together.
6. Mix in flour to thicken, as desired.
7. Peel the pearl onions and wash well with water. Boil them in a deep pan for 15 minutes until cooked.
8. Peel and chop the three remaining carrots and the potatoes into rectangular shapes.
9. In another deep pan, boil the carrots and potatoes for 10 minutes.
10. Using a sieve, drain the water from both the pan with the onions and the pan with the carrots and potatoes.
11. Add the onions, carrots, potatoes, and meat to the brown sauce, and stir for 5 minutes on low heat.
12. Transfer to a *tagin* and heat in the oven for 5 minutes before serving.

Serve with white rice.

800g / 1¾ lb boneless veal

180ml / ¾ cup corn oil

1 tsp salt

1 tsp white pepper

1 beef stock cube

1 large onion (about 100g / 3½ oz)

3 cardamom pods

1 bunch celery, chopped

4 carrots (about 500g / 1 lb), 1 grated for the brown sauce and 3 chopped for the stew

1 tomato (about 200g / 7 oz), peeled and grated

2 tbsp flour

12 pearl onions (about 250g / ½ lb)

3 medium-sized potatoes (about 500g / 1 lb)

1 liter / 4 cups beef stock

¼ tsp ground cinnamon

Pearl onions are sweetly flavored, more so than other types of onions, and are used in many cuisines.

White Bean Tagin

Abou El Sid Style

Serves: 2 - 4 | Preparation time: 45 minutes

Preheat the oven to 180°C / 350°F.

Preparing the meat

1: In a pan, boil the meat (both the veal cubes and sausages), celery, cardamom pods, white pepper, and salt for 30 minutes.
2. Slice 1 onion lengthwise and add to the pan. For extra seasoning, add a beef stock cube.
3. Drain the meat with a sieve, and set it aside. Keep the meat stock to use with the red sauce.

Preparing the white beans

4. Boil in 4 cups of water for 25 minutes.
5. Drain the white peas with a sieve, and set them aside to use in the red sauce.

Preparing the red sauce

6. Grate the remaining onion. Heat it in a pan with corn oil and the chopped garlic, stirring until they turn brown.
7. Add the tomatoes and carrots to the pan.
8. Add the cardamom pods, salt, and pepper.
9. Cook for 15 minutes. Add flour to thicken the sauce, as desired.
10. Add the white beans to the red sauce and stir until cooked, about 15 minutes.
11. Add the cooked meat at the very end and mix together.
12. Transfer to a *tagin*, and heat in oven for 10 minutes.

Serve with white rice.

500g / 1 lb veal, cut into cubes 4cm x 4cm / 2 in x 2 in

250g / ½ lb sausages

1 celery stalk, chopped

2 cardamom pods

½ tsp white pepper

1 tsp salt

2 large onions (about 250g / ½ lb)

1 beef stock cube

5 medium tomatoes (about 500g / 1 lb), peeled and grated

4 carrots (about 500g / 1 lb), grated

2 tbsp flour

500g / 1 lb white beans

2 tbsp corn oil

5 garlic cloves (about 100g), chopped

Abou El Sid's recipe for this tagin is unique, as it uses two different kinds of meat: veal and sausages. When served with rice, it is considered a full meal rather than a side dish.

Roasted Veal Abou El Sid Style

Serves: 2 - 4 | Preparation time: 60 minutes

Preheat the oven to 180°C / 350°F.

Preparing the meat

1. Cut the veal into cubes 4cm x 4cm (1½ inches x 1½ inches).
2. Spread a little oil on a baking sheet.
3. Put the meat, tomatoes, carrots, garlic, celery, bay leaves, cardamom pods, black pepper, and salt on the sheet. For extra seasoning, add mixed spices.
4. Cook in the oven for 30 minutes.
5. When done, separate the meat from the vegetables.
6. Pureé the vegetables in a blender and sieve the mixture to extract the juices.
7. Heat the juices in a deep pan over medium heat, and add the meat and half of the saffron.

Preparing the rice

8. Wash the rice very well.
9. Heat 4 tbsp oil in a deep pan.
10. Add 1 grated onion, and stir until it turns light golden.
11. Add the rice and the remaining saffron, and stir.
12. Add 1½ cups water. Simmer over low heat for 15 minutes.

Serve the meat and rice together.

500g / 1 lb boneless veal

250ml / 1 cup corn oil

2 medium tomatoes (about 250 g / ½ lb), chopped

3 carrots (about 250g / ½ lb), chopped

4 cloves garlic, finely chopped or pressed

1 bunch celery, chopped

2 bay leaves

6 cardamom pods

½ tsp black pepper

½ tsp salt

1 tsp mixed spices

pinch of saffron, or 2 tsp turmeric if saffron is not available

1 medium-sized onion, grated

500g / 2 cups rice

This dish is a specialty of Abou El Sid. It can be cooked with turmeric if saffron is not available.

Green Peas Tagin

Serves: 2 - 4 | Preparation time: 45 minutes

Preheat the oven to 180°C/ 350°F.

Preparing the meat
1. Boil the meat, celery, cardamom pods, white pepper, and salt for 30 minutes.
2. Slice 1 onion into rounds. Add onion and garlic to the pan. For extra seasoning, add a beef stock cube.
3. Drain the meat with a sieve, and put it aside. Keep the meat stock to use with the red sauce.

Preparing the red sauce
4. Grate remaining onion and heat in a pan with the corn oil. Stir until they turn brown.
5. Peel and chop the tomatoes, and add to the pan. Add the salt and pepper. Cook for 15 minutes. Add flour to thicken, as desired.

6. Finely and evenly chop the carrots, and add to the red sauce.
7. Add the green peas, and stir until cooked, about 15 minutes.
8. Stir in the cooked meat at the very end.
9. Transfer to a *tagin* and heat in the oven for 10 minutes.

Serve with white rice.

500g / 1 lb veal

1 celery stalk (about 100g / 3½ oz)

2 cardamom pods

½ tsp white pepper

1 tsp salt

5 garlic cloves, chopped fine

2 large onions (about 250g / ½ lb)

1 beef stock cube

2 tbsp corn oil

5 medium tomatoes (about 500g / 1 lb)

4 carrots (about 500g / 1 lb)

2 tbsp flour

500g / 1 lb fresh green peas

When served with rice, this dish is considered a full meal.

Veal Tagin with Shaareya

Serves: 2 - 4 | Preparation time: 40 minutes

Preheat the oven to 100°C / 212°F.

Preparing the *shaareya*

1: Fry the *shaareya* in oil, and add ½ tsp salt, ½ tsp pepper, and ground cinnamon. Stir until it turns a dark golden brown.
2. Drain the oil from the *shaareya*, using a sieve.

Preparing the veal

3. Dust the meat with flour.
4. In the oil from the *shaareya*, fry the meat with one chopped onion until it turns dark golden brown.
5. Boil 4 cups of water in a pot.
6. Drop in the fried veal and onions, and cook for 30 minutes. Add ½ tsp salt, ½ tsp pepper, and, for extra seasoning, a beef stock cube.
7. Drain the meat with a sieve, and put it aside.
8. Keep 1 cup of the meat broth to use later.

Preparing the brown meat sauce

9. In another pan, heat the other chopped onion in corn oil, stirring until it turns dark brown.
10. Stir in the cardamom pods, ½ tsp. salt, ½ tsp. pepper, carrot, and tomato with the cup of broth left from cooking the meat.
11. Mix in flour to thicken, as desired.
12. Place in a *tagin*, putting the *shaareya* at the bottom, then the meat, and finally the brown sauce. Heat in the oven for 10 minutes before serving.

800g / 1¾ lb boneless veal

180ml / ¾ cup corn oil

1 tsp salt

1 tsp white pepper

1 beef stock cube

225g / 1 cup *shaareya*

¼ tsp ground cinnamon

2 medium onions (about 250g /
   ½ lb), chopped

3 cardamom pods

1 carrot (about 75g / 2½ oz),
   grated

1 tomato (about 200g / 7 oz),
   peeled and grated

2 tbsp flour

―――――――――――――――――

Shaareya is short, thin vermicelli pasta.

Molokheya

Serves: 2 - 4 | Preparation time: 25 minutes

Making the chicken stock

1. Wash and clean the chicken very well with flour and salt.
2. Add the chicken, bay leaves, cardamom pods, celery, salt, 2 tsp coriander, and sliced onions to a pan of boiling water. Cook for 30 minutes.
3. When cooked, remove the chicken and vegetables, reserving the chicken to serve with the *molokheya*, if desired.
4. Put 3 cups of the chicken stock in a pan and add the *molokheya*. On medium heat, stir continuously to make sure the *molokheya* absorbs the stock. Do not allow it to boil.
5. In another pan, heat crushed garlic in corn oil, stirring till it turns golden. Then add 1 tsp of crushed coriander, and stir with the garlic.
6. Toss in the hot *molokheya*, and you will hear "tshhhh." This is known as *tasha* in Arabic.

Preparing the red sauce

7. Grate the onions, and heat in a pan with corn oil until they turn brown.
8. Peel and chop the tomatoes, saving the juice.
9. Add tomatoes, tomato juice, and tomato paste to the pan. Cook for 15 minutes.

Molokheya can be served on its own with white rice, or with red sauce and chicken, rabbit, or meatballs (see pp. 101, 103, 105). It is also often served with finely chopped onions and vinegar.

2 whole chickens (about 3kg / 6½ lbs)

2 tbsp flour

2 bay leaves

4 cardamom pods

2 celery stalks (about 200g / 7 oz)

½ tsp salt

1 tbsp coriander leaves, finely chopped

500g / 1lb *molokheya*

4 small onions (about 200g / 7 oz)

5 garlic cloves, crushed

3 tbsp corn oil

3 large tomatoes (about 600g / 21 oz)

2 tbsp tomato paste

The Arabic word for Egypt's national dish molokheya is a derivative of the word mulukiya, which literally means 'kingly' or 'of the kings.' The English name for this plant is Jew's mallow, jute mallow, or nalta—not to be confused with mallow leaf. In Egypt, fresh molokheya leaves are removed from the stems, and then minced by hand using a vegetable chopper that is an arched blade with two vertical handles.

Molokheya with Chicken

Serves: 2 - 4 | Preparation time: 45 minutes

Preparing the chicken

1. Soak the chickens for 10 minutes in warm salted water.
2. Using a knife, clean and remove the skin and bones. Rub the chicken with salt to clean it. Rinse with warm water.
3. Boil 2 liters of water in a pot, and add the chickens to it. Add the bay leaves, cardamom pods, salt, and pepper.
4. Cook for 30 minutes.
5. Remove the chicken from the stock.
6. Mix the chicken in tomato paste.
7. In another pan, heat the corn oil and butter.
8. Fry the chicken till it turns reddish gold.

Serve with *molokheya* (see p. 99) and white rice.

2 chickens (about 3kg / 6½ lbs)

3 bay leaves

4 cardamom pods

2 tsp salt

½ tsp black pepper

2 small onions (about 100g / 3½ oz), sliced

4 tbsp corn oil

1 tbsp butter

1 tbsp tomato paste

This chicken dish is served with molokheya, the Egyptian national dish.

Molokheya with Rabbit

Serves: 2 - 4 | Preparation time: 55 minutes

Preparing the rabbits

1. Soak the rabbits for 10 minutes in warm salted water.
2. Using a knife, remove the skin and bones. Rub the rabbits with salt to clean them. Wash with warm water to remove any excess salt.
3. Boil 2 liters / 8 cups water in a pot, and add the rabbit to it.
4. Add the bay leaves, cardamom pods, celery, salt, pepper, and sliced onions.
5. Cook for 30 minutes.
6. Remove the rabbit from the stock. (This broth can be used to make the *molokheya*).
7. Mix rabbits in tomato paste.
8. In a pan, heat the corn oil and butter.
9. Fry the rabbits until they become reddish gold.

Serve with *molokheya* (see p. 99) and white rice.

2 rabbits (about 2kg / 4.5 lb cleaned)

3 bay leaves

4 cardamom pods

1 celery stalk

2 tsp salt

½ tsp black pepper

2 small onions (about 100g / 3½ oz), sliced

4 tbsp corn oil

1 tbsp butter

1 tbsp tomato paste

Rabbits are often served with molokheya, the Egyptian national dish, and topped with red sauce.

Molokheya with Meatballs

in Red Sauce

Serves: 2 - 4 | Preparation time: 25 minutes

Preparing the meatballs

1. Mix both types of meat, 1 grated onion, ½ tsp salt, ¼ tsp black pepper, nutmeg, and cinnamon in a food processor, until well combined.
2. Using the palms of your hands, roll the mixture into balls 3cm / 1¼ in. in diameter.
3. Heat the corn oil in a pan on medium heat, and fry the meatballs until they become golden brown.

Preparing the red sauce

4. Sauté the remaining onion and the chopped garlic in a pan over medium heat until they brown.
5. Add the tomatoes, tomato paste, bay leaves, ½ tsp salt, and ¼ tsp pepper. Cook for 15 minutes, stirring constantly.

6. Combine the red sauce and the meatballs, and serve with *molokheya* (see p. 99) and white rice.

250g / ½ lb ground beef

250g / ½ lb ground veal

2 small onions (about 100g / 3½ oz), grated

1 tsp salt

½ tsp black pepper

¼ tsp ground nutmeg

¼ tsp ground cinnamon

4 tbsp corn oil

4 large tomatoes (about 800g / 1¾ lb), peeled and grated

4 cardamom pods

5 garlic cloves, chopped

1 tbsp tomato paste

3 bay leaves

These meatballs, served here as a side dish with molokheya, are known as dawoud basha. Abou El Sid mixes two different kinds of meat together to produce a more tender meatball.

Stuffed Pigeon with Rice or Fireek

Serves: 2 - 4 | Preparation time: 1 hour, 15 minutes.

Preparing the rice
1. Wash the rice well.
2. In a bowl, mix the rice, 1 grated onion, dried mint, black pepper, and salt.

Preparing the *fireek*
3. Wash the *fireek* and soak it for 30 minutes.
4. Heat oil and butter in a deep pan. Add the onions, black pepper, and salt; stir until the onions turn golden brown.
5. Add the *fireek* and ¼ cup water. Stir over low heat for 10 minutes.
6. Remove from the heat, and allow to cool before stuffing the pigeons.

Preparing the pigeons
7. Remove wings. Using scissors, remove legs and knees. Remove the heads and tails, by cutting as close to the to the pigeon's body as possible. Remove the skin and feathers. Remove the intestines, lungs, and heart.
8. Stuff the pigeons with the rice or *fireek* mix. Close the rear end of the pigeon with toothpicks to keep the rice or *fireek* from falling out.
9. In a deep pan boil 1½ liters / 6 cups water, and add the celery, bay leaves, cardamom pods, and the two remaining onions, chopped.
10. Boil the pigeons for 1 hour.
11. Remove the pigeons and fry in a pan with oil for 5 minutes, until they brown.
12. Remove the toothpicks.

Serve hot.

500g / 2 cups rice or *fireek* (dried green wheat)

3 large onions (about 500g / 1 lb), grated

1 tsp dried mint

1 tsp black pepper

2 tsp salt

4 pigeons

1 bunch celery

2 bay leaves

4 cardamom pods

500ml / 2 cups corn oil

Stuffed pigeons are one of Egypt's most popular dishes. Although preparing this dish may seem daunting to those not familiar with Egyptian cuisine, once the pigeons are clean, it is easy and fast. The green wheat known as fireek is used widely in Egypt, but is fairly uncommon outside the Middle East. The seeds are removed during harvesting, when they are still soft, then sun-dried. Rice can be used instead, but fireek has a uniquely crunchy texture.

Circassian Chicken with Walnut Sauce

Serves: 2 - 4 | Preparation time: 1 hour

Preparing the chicken

1. Soak the chicken for 10 minutes in warm salted water. Using a knife, remove the chicken skin, and the bones.
2. Rub the chicken all over with salt to clean it further, and rinse with warm water.
3. In a pan, bring 2 liters of water to boil, and add the chicken.
4. Add the bay leaves, cardamom pods, celery, salt, pepper, 1 tbsp coriander, chopped carrot, and 1 crushed onion. Cook for 30 minutes.
5. Strain the chicken from the stock and reserve.

Preparing the Circassian sauce

6. Soak the walnuts and slices of toasted bread in milk for 15 minutes. Pureé in a blender until the texture is very smooth.
7. In a deep pan combine 3 cups of chicken stock, 2 sliced onions, salt, white pepper, and butter. Stir for 5 minutes.
8. Add the walnut mixture, and stir for 10 minutes.
9. If mixture is not thick enough, add flour until the mixture is a bit thicker than syrup.
10. In another pan, combine 2 of the chopped garlic cloves with the corn oil and coriander, and heat while stirring until it turns golden. When it boils, add the Circassian sauce, and you will hear "tshhhh." This is known as *tasha* in Arabic.

Preparing the red sauce

11. Chop tomatoes fine, and heat in a pan with a little oil and the 2 remaining garlic cloves. Sauté until they turn brown.
12. Peel the tomato, mix with the tomato paste, and add to the pan.
13. Add the salt and pepper. Cook, stirring, over medium-low heat for 15 minutes.

14. On a serving plate, add white rice, then the Circassian sauce, and the chicken on top. Serve the red sauce on the side.

1 whole chicken
3 bay leaves
4 cardamom pods
1 bunch celery
2 tsp salt
½ tsp black pepper
1½ tbsp ground coriander
1 carrot, chopped small
3 medium onions (about 250g / ½ lb)
250g / ½ lb walnuts
4 slices toasted bread
500ml / 2 cups milk
1 tbsp butter
3 tbsp flour
4 garlic cloves, finely chopped
1 tbsp corn oil
4 large tomatoes (about 800g / 1¾ lbs)
2 garlic cloves
1 tbsp tomato paste
500g / 2½ cups white rice

Circassian chicken is one of the old Turkish recipes that have been adapted for Egyptian cuisine throughout the years. It is a nourishing, rich dish of chicken, creamy walnut sauce, rice, and special red sauces. It is often served as a main dish at Egyptian feasts.

Grilled Veal Chops

Serves: 2 - 4 | Preparation time: 1 hour

Marinating the veal chops

1. Peel the tomato and 1 onion, and pureé them.
2. Strain the juice, and add the salt, white pepper, and mixed spices.
3. Add the veal, and marinate for 15 minutes.

Preparing the rice

4. Finely chop the 2 remaining onions and fry in a pan with 3 tbsp corn oil until browned.
5. Add 3 cups of water and stir.
6. Wash rice and put in a different pot with 3 tbsp corn oil.
7. Add the fried onions and water to the rice. Simmer on low heat for 15 minutes, until the water is absorbed.

Grilling the veal

8. Grill the veal chops, pouring the remaining marinating sauce over them.

Serve with rice, sprinkled with mixed nuts.

1 medium tomato (about 100g / 3½ oz)

3 medium onions (about 250g / 9 oz)

½ tsp salt

¼ tsp white pepper

2 tsp mixed spices

1 kg / 2 lb veal chops

90ml / 6 tbsp corn oil

500g / 2½ cups rice

150g / 5 oz chopped mixed nuts (almonds and hazelnuts) and raisins

_____

Grilled veal is a recipe prepared in many different cuisines. Abou El Sid's grilled veal chops are marinated in a delicious and easy-to-prepare way.

Abou El Sid Tournedos Fillet

with Chicken Liver and Vegetables

Serves: 2 - 4 | Preparation time: 45 minutes

Preheat grill and oven to 160°C / 320°.

Brown sauce

1. Sauté the corn oil, ½ tbsp butter, chopped onion, and minced garlic over medium heat, stirring, until it turns dark brown.
2. Add the cardamom pods, chopped celery, salt, pepper, and grated carrot with 1 cup water, and stir all together.
3. Stir in flour until sauce reaches the desired thickness.

Chicken livers

4. Rinse the chicken livers well with water. Cut them into cubes 1.5cm x 1.5cm (about ½ inch x ½ inch).
5. Heat the pan on high with corn oil, add the chicken livers, and stir until cooked, about 10 minutes.

Fillet preparation

6. Brush the beef with the corn oil, then grill on both sides until done.
7. Heat the beef in the brown sauce for 5 minutes.
8. Add the chicken liver to the beef in sauce and heat for 5 minutes.

Bread preparation

9. Cut the toast in circles with a diameter of about 5cm / 2 inches.

Vegetable preparation

10. Cut the potatoes and zucchini in rectangular slices.
11. Cut the green beans in half.
12. Boil the vegetables in water for 15 minutes, and drain.
13. In a pan, heat ½ tbsp butter with the salt, then pour over the vegetables.

To serve, place a toast round on a plate, top it with a fillet, and place a chicken liver on top. Repeat with remaining fillets and livers. Serve with vegetables on the side.

3 tbsp corn oil

1 tbsp butter

1 large onion (about 150g / 5 oz), chopped

2 garlic cloves, minced

2 cardamom pods

2 tbsp chopped celery

¼ tsp salt

¼ tsp black pepper

4 medium carrots (about 200g / 7 oz), grated

1 tbsp flour

250g / ½ lb chicken livers

800g / 1¾ lb beef fillet

4 slices toasted bread

200g / 7 oz green beans

2 large potatoes (about 200g / 7 oz)

3 medium zucchini (about 200g / 7 oz)

This dish was created at Abou El Sid's restaurants. It is known for its delicious taste and unique combination of chicken livers with beef fillet.

Koshari

Serves: 2 - 4 | Preparation time: 1 hour, 30 minutes

1. Fry half of the onions in a pan with corn oil over medium heat until they turn golden.
2. Drain the onions, and place on paper towels to absorb the excess oil.
3. Wash the lentils and chickpeas, and soak in water for 30 minutes.
4. Boil the chickpeas for 30 minutes and the lentils for 15 minutes until cooked.
5. Boil the spaghetti in water with ¼ tsp oil for 11 minutes, or until al dente. Drain.
6. In another pan, fry the *shaareya*, and stir until it turns golden.
7. Then add the ditalini.
8. Add 1½ cups of water, bring to a boil, and reduce heat to simmer on low heat for 15 minutes, and drain.
9. Wash rice and add to a pan with a little oil. Add 1 cup water, bring to a boil, then reduce heat and simmer for 10 minutes until the water is absorbed.
10. Once the rice is cooked, mix it with the lentils, chickpeas, spaghetti, and ditalini and transfer to a serving plate. Keep warm.

Preparing the red sauce
11. Finely chop the remaining onions, and sauté in oil over medium heat until they brown.
12. Peel and chop the tomato, and add it to the pan with the tomato paste.
13. Add the cardamom pods, salt, and pepper. Cook for 10 minutes.
14. In another pan, sauté the garlic with the corn oil and vinegar, and heat while stirring until it turns golden brown. Add the red sauce, and you will hear "tshhhh." This is known as *tasha* in Arabic.
15. Add chili powder (optional).

Garnish with crispy fried onions, and serve with plain or spicy tomato sauce on the side, according to your preference.

500g / 1 lb onions, thinly sliced
125ml / ½ cup corn oil
150g / 5 oz brown lentils
150g / 5 oz dried chickpeas
150g / 5 oz spaghetti
150g / 5 oz *shaareya* (vermicelli pasta)
150g / 5 oz ditalini pasta
200g / 7 oz rice
5 medium tomatoes (about 300g / 10 oz)
1 tbsp tomato paste
3 cardamom pods
1 tsp salt
1/8 tsp white pepper
5 garlic cloves, finely chopped
2 tbsp vinegar
½ tsp chili powder (optional)

Eating koshari is living like a real Egyptian. It is a vegetarian dish, one that could be served to the family at the end of the month if rations were spare. It is prepared in every home, and is also sold at Egyptian street stands.

Fish Sayadeya

Serves: 2 - 4 | Preparation time: 1 hour

Preheat oven to 160°C / 320°F.

Fish preparation
1. Wash the fish, and cut it into cubes 3cm x 3cm / 1¼ inches x 1¼ inches.
2. Combine the chili, ½ tsp salt, ½ tsp cumin, lemon juice, and minced garlic. Add the fish, and marinate for 15 minutes.
3. Drain the fish, dust with flour, and fry over low heat for 10 minutes until it turns golden brown.

Rice
4. Fry 2 chopped onions in a small pan until they turn light golden brown.
5. Purée 2 of the tomatoes, add them and the tomato paste to the onions, and continue stirring.
6. Add the rice, 2 cups of water, and ½ tsp salt, stir, and cook on low heat for 15 minutes.

Sayadeya sauce preparation
7. In a pan, sauté the 3 remaining onions in 2 tbsp oil until they turn golden brown.
8. Dice the four remaining tomatoes into cubes about 1.5cm x 1.5cm / ½ in x ½ in. Add grated carrots, green peppers, and cardamom pods. Cook for 5 minutes.
9. Add the marinade that was drained from the fish.
10. Serve in a *tagin*, putting in the rice first, then fish, then the *sayadeya* sauce.
11. Heat in the oven for 5 minutes before serving.

Serve with *tahina*.

600g / 1¼ lb firm white fish such as haddock or cod
½ tsp chili
1 tsp salt
1 tsp cumin
juice of 3 lemons
4 garlic cloves
2 tbsp flour
¼ cup corn oil
5 medium onions (about 500g / 1 lb), diced
6 medium tomatoes (about 500g / 1 lb), peeled and diced about 1.5cm x 1.5cm / ½ in x ½ in
1 tbsp tomato paste
500g / 2½ cups rice
2 medium carrots (about 250g / ½ lb), grated
3 medium green bell peppers (about 250g / ½ lb), diced about 1.5cm x 1.5cm / ½ in x ½ in
3 cardamom pods

Besides being delicious, this recipe is a healthy dish in the Egyptian cuisine.

Grilled Fish

Serves: 2 - 4 | Preparation time: 30 minutes

Preheat the grill.

Fish preparation
1. Wash and cut the fish into slices 8cm / 3 inches long.
2. Marinate fish in ½ tsp salt, cumin, lemon juice, and minced garlic for 5 minutes.
3. Drain the fish, reserving the marinade.
4. Put the extra marinade in a pan over low heat.
5. Brush the corn oil onto the fish, and grill for 5 minutes (2½
6. minutes each side).
7. Remove fish from grill, and heat in the extra marinade for 5 minutes.

Rice
8. Fry the onions in a small pan until they turn light golden brown.
9. Peel the tomatoes, pureé them, add the tomatoes and the tomato paste to the onions, and continue stirring.
10. Add rice, ½ tsp salt, and 2¼ cups water. Stir, and cook over low heat for 15 minutes.

Serve the fish hot with the rice, with *tahina* on the side.

600g / 1¼ lb firm white fish such as haddock or cod

1 tsp salt

½ tsp cumin

juice of 3 lemons (about 125ml / 4 oz)

4 garlic cloves

4 tbsp corn oil

3 medium onions, diced

3 medium tomatoes

1 tbsp tomato paste

500g / 2½ cups rice

2¼ cups water

This is a light and healthy Egyptian dish.

Shrimp Tagin with Red Rice

Serves: 2 - 4 | Preparation time: 30 minutes

Preheat oven to 180°C / 350°F.

Preparing the rice
1. Finely chop one of the onions and fry in oil until brown.
2. Peel and chop 3 of the tomatoes, and blend with the onions.
3. Add the tomato paste to the mixture and keep stirring.
4. Add the rice and salt, stir, and cook on low heat for 15 minutes.

Preparing the shrimp sauce
Always keep the shrimp cold while working.
5. Pull off the heads and legs. With a knife, cut the outer edge of the shell on the back. Remove the vein. Wash them well.
6. Dice the other onion and add to a deep pan with the corn oil and garlic. Stir until the onions turn a golden color.
7. Peel and chop the rest of the tomatoes, and stir into the pan.
8. Add the shrimps, salt, chili, and cumin and simmer for 5 minutes on low heat. Do not allow the mixture to dry out.
9. Place in a *tagin*, adding the rice first, and then the shrimp with the sauce on top. Heat in the oven for 5 minutes before serving.

Garnish with finely chopped parsley.

2 large onions (about 250g / ½ lb)

6 medium tomatoes (about 500g / 1 lb)

1 tbsp tomato paste

800g / 1¾ lb shrimp

250ml / 1 cup corn oil

4 garlic cloves, finely chopped

2 cups rice

1 tsp salt

¼ tsp chili

½ tsp ground cumin

½ bunch parsley

Seafood Tagin with Red Rice

Serves: 2 - 4 | Preparation time: 1 hour

Preheat oven to 160°C / 320°F.

Preparing the seafood

1. Wash and cut fish into cubes of around 3cm x 3cm / 1¼ inches x 1¼ inches.
2. Pull the squid's head gently to remove the organ. Reach into the mantle to remove it completely.
3. Scrape the outer surface of the mantle using a sharp knife. Cut the mantle in cubes 2cm x 2cm / 1½ inches x 1½ inches, and wash.
4. Keep the shrimps cold while working. Pull off the heads and legs.
5. With a knife, cut the outer edge of the shrimp's back. Remove the vein and wash well.
6. Mix all of the seafood with the chili, ½ tsp. salt, ½ tsp. cumin, lemon juice, and 3 cloves garlic. Marinate for 15 minutes.
7. Cover only the fish in flour and fry on low heat for 10 minutes until it turn a golden color.
8. In another pan, brown 1 garlic clove in oil. Add the shrimps and squid, and stir for 3 minutes on medium heat.

Preparing the rice

9. Dice 4 onions and fry in oil until they turn light golden brown.
10. Peel and blend half of the tomatoes, add them and the tomato paste to the pan, and keep stirring.
11. Add the rice, 2 cups water, and ½ tsp salt.
12. Stir together and cook on low heat for 15 minutes.

Preparing the sauce

13. Dice the remaining onion and put in a deep pan with 2 tbsp corn oil. Heat until the onions turn golden brown.
14. Peel and finely chop the rest of the tomatoes. Add them and the grated carrots to the pan. Finely chop the green bell peppers and add with the cardamom pods and stir.
15. Place in a *tagin*, by layering the seafood over the rice and pouring the sauce over the top. Heat in the oven for 5 minutes before serving. Serve with *tahina*.

300g / 11 oz firm white fish, such as haddock or cod

300g / 11 oz squid

200g / 7 oz shrimps

½ tsp chili

1 tsp salt

1 tsp ground cumin

juice of 3 lemons (about 125ml / 4½ oz)

4 garlic cloves, pressed

2 tbsp flour

500ml / 2 cups corn oil

5 medium-sized onions (about 500g / 1 lb)

400g / 2 cups rice

6 medium-sized tomatoes (about 500g / 1 lb)

1 tbsp tomato paste

2 medium carrots, grated (about 250g / ½ lb)

3 medium green bell peppers (about 250g / ½ lb)

3 cardamom pods

Fettah

Egyptian rice with yogurt, meat, and tomato sauce

Serves: 2 - 4 | Preparation time: 45 minutes

Meat preparation

1. Put the meat, celery, 1 chopped carrot, 1 cardamom pod, ½ tsp salt, and ¼ tsp white pepper in a saucepan with 5 cups water to boil for half hour until cooked. For extra seasoning, add a beef stock cube.
2. Drain the meat with a sieve. Put the meat broth aside to use with the red sauce preparation.
3. In a pan, heat 4 tbsp corn oil with the tomato paste, and add the meat, cooking it until it turns a bronze color from the tomato sauce. Remove the meat from the oil, and season with salt and pepper.

White rice preparation

4. Rinse and drain the rice. Heat 2 tbsp corn oil in a pan, over medium heat, and add the rice. Stir for 5 minutes.
5. Add 2 cups of water and 1 tsp salt and continue stirring. Lower the heat, cover the pan, and cook for 10 minutes, until all the water is absorbed.

Bread preparation

6. Cut pita bread loaves into squares 2cm x 2cm.
7. Heat butter in pan, and fry the bread in it until it turns dark gold.
8. In a different pan, sauté the crushed garlic with corn oil until it turns golden brown. Add the vinegar and meat broth, and bring to a boil. Toss in the bread squares, and you will hear "tshhhh." This is known as *tasha* in Arabic.

Preparing the red sauce

9. Sauté the chopped onions in a pan with 2 tbsps oil until browned.
10. Peel and chop the tomatoes. Add to the pan with the grated carrot, the 2 remaining cardamom pods, ½ tsp salt, and ¼ tsp pepper. Sauté for about 15 minutes. Gradually stir in enough flour to thicken the sauce to the desired consistency.
11. Mix the yogurt with the chopped garlic until well blended.
12. Line the bottom of a deep dish with pieces of bread.
13. Add the yogurt on top of the bread.
14. Add a layer of red sauce, then the rice with the rest of the vinegar sauce, then another layer of red sauce, ending with the meat. Serve.

600g / 1¼ lb boned veal shank

1 celery stalk

2 medium-sized carrots
(about 150g)—one chopped,
one grated

3 cardamom pods

2 tsp salt

½ tsp white pepper

1 beef stock cube

8 tbsp corn oil

2 tbsp tomato paste

500g / 2 cups rice

2 loaves pita bread

1 tbsp butter

2 crushed garlic cloves

2 chopped garlic cloves

1 tbsp vinegar

250g / ½ lb onions

500g / 1 lb tomatoes

2 tbsp flour

250ml / 1 cup yogurt

Abou El Sid fettah is made with Egyptian rice, a short-grained, starchy variety, and yogurt, meat, and tomato sauce. This recipe uses the traditional Egyptian pita bread. The bread should be toasted before serving.

Mixed Grill

Serves: 2 - 4 | Preparation time: 30 minutes

Preheat the grill.

Preparing the *kofta*
1. Mix the ground beef and the fat with 1 grated onion, ½ tsp salt, ¼ tsp white pepper, mixed spices, and corn oil to create a dough-like consistency.
2. Using your hands, mold the mixture into cylindrical shapes 4cm x 7cm / 1½ inches x 3 inches.

Preparing the marinade
3. Peel the tomatoes and 1 onion, and grate thoroughly. Sieve them so as to use only the juices.
4. Add mustard, salt, white pepper, and corn oil.

Preparing the veal ribs, veal *kebab* brochette, and shish tawouk brochette
5. Cut the veal *kebab* and *shish tawouk* into cubes, 4cm x 4cm / 1½ inches x 1½ inches.
6. Chop 2 onions and the green peppers into cubes, 3cm x 3cm / 1¼ inches x 1¼ inches.
7. Put onion, green pepper, and veal *kebab* or *shish tawouk* onto a wooden stick, in that order. Repeat until there are 3 of each item on every stick.
8. Put the veal *kebab* sticks, *shish tawouk* sticks, and veal ribs in the sauce to marinate for 10 minutes.
9. Smear the *kofta*, veal ribs, veal *kebab* brochettes, and *shish tawouk* brochettes with oil, so they don't stick on the grill while cooking.
10. Grill until cooked according to your taste.

Serve with Egyptian *baladi* bread and tahina.

500g / 1 lb ground beef
¼ kg / ½ lb minced lamb fat
200g / 7 oz veal kebab
4 onions (1/2 kg / 1 lb)
1 tsp salt
1 tsp white pepper
½ tsp mixed spices
1 tbsp corn oil
4 pieces veal ribs (400g / 1 lb)
400g / 14 oz *shish tawouk*
  (boned chicken chunks)
2 tomatoes
1 tsp mustard
2 green peppers
wooden or metal skewers

desserts

Om Ali with Mixed Nuts

Serves: 2 - 4 | Preparation time: 30 minutes

1. Preheat oven to 160° C / 320° F.
2. Butter a baking sheet, and place the puff pastry on it. Bake until the top layer turns golden and crunchy, and remove from oven.
3. In a bowl, mix the raisins, almonds, hazelnuts, and vanilla.
4. Break the pastry into little pieces and put in the bottom of the *tagin*.
5. Add the nut mixture.
6. Bring the milk to a boil in a saucepan over medium heat while adding the sugar and stirring. Remove from heat.
7. Whip the heavy cream.
8. Add the boiled milk to the *tagin*, add whipped cream on top, and bake in the oven for 10 minutes.
9. Sprinkle the pistachios on the top, and serve.

½ package/ 8.75 oz frozen puff pastry sheets, thawed

4 tbsp sugar

125g / 5 oz raisins

100g / 3½ oz almonds, chopped

100g / 3½ oz hazelnuts, chopped

1 packet vanilla powder (¼ tsp)

500ml / 2 cups milk

100g / 3½ oz pistachios, finely chopped

180 ml / ¾ cup heavy cream

The literal translation of this delectable dessert is 'Ali's Mother.' It is served at Abou El Sid in a tagin.

Mohalabeya
Oriental Milk Pudding

Serves: 2 - 4 | Preparation time: 20 minutes

1. Wash the rice and soak in water for 10 minutes.
2. Drain the rice, and pulverize or grind it using mortar and pestle or blender. Put the rice and ½ cup of water into a deep pan.
3. Add the milk and stir for 15 minutes, adding sugar and vanilla as you stir. Simmer on low heat until rice is cooked.
4. In a bowl, mix the cornstarch with ¼ cup of water, and stir until completely mixed.
5. Add gradually to the rice, stirring while pouring.
6. Transfer to a serving bowl and leave to cool, then refrigerate until serving.
7. Sprinkle finely chopped mixed nuts and raisins on top before serving.

1 tbsp rice

120ml / ½ cup water

60ml / ¼ cup water, separately

500ml / 2 cups milk

4 tbsp sugar

1 packet / ¼ tsp vanilla powder

3 tbsp cornstarch

20g / 1 oz raisins

20g / 1 oz almonds, finely chopped

20g / 1 oz hazelnuts, finely chopped

20g / 1 oz pistachios, finely chopped

This dessert is the Egyptian milk pudding, the favorite of almost every Egyptian child.

Fiteer Meshaltet

Oriental Pancakes

Serves: 2 - 4 | Preparation time: 1 hour, 15 minutes

1. Preheat oven to 200°C / 400°F.
2. In a bowl, mix flour, salt, and ½ cup water, pouring the water slowly to avoid stickiness.
3. Keep stirring until the dough is smooth and elastic.
4. Knead for 15 minutes by machine, or by hand.
5. Divide the dough into 4 equal parts and press with the hands to remove excess air.
6. Shape into four 5cm / 2 inch diameter circles.
7. Brush with melted butter and set aside for 5 minutes.
8. Roll out each round of the dough with a rolling pin on a flat surface to 30 cm / 12 inches in diameter.
9. Brush the dough with oil and place on a greased baking sheet, one on top of the other.
10. Bake for 20 minutes or until browned.
11. Remove from the oven and cut into triangular slices.

Best served hot with white honey, black honey, or heavy fresh cream, and mixed nuts.

480g / 4 cups flour

1 tsp salt

120 ml / ½ cup water

4 tbsp sugar

100g / 3½ oz ground mixed nuts

½ kg / 1 lb butter

6 tbsp corn oil

4 tbsp white honey, black honey, or heavy fresh cream

This dessert is a favorite Egyptian treat. The dough can be kept in the refrigerator for 4 days (brushed with butter), and baked fresh. Egyptians eat it with honey and fresh cream according to their preference. The fiteer can be served as a savory dish with cheese or sausages.

Ashoura with Mixed Nuts

Serves: 2 - 4 | Preparation time: 2 hours

1. Soak the whole wheat grain in a pan with the warm water for 1 hour, then cook on low heat for 40 minutes until all the water is absorbed.
2. Add the milk, sugar, rosewater, cornstarch, raisins, pistachios, and almonds.
3. Stir until all is combined well, and cook further until the mixture thickens.
4. Transfer to a serving plate, and allow to cool. Sprinkle some whole pistachios decoratively over the *'ashoura*.

110g / ½ cup whole wheat grain (wheat berries)

3 cups warm water

360ml / 1½ cups milk

4 tbsp sugar

1 tsp rosewater

1 tsp cornstarch

20g / 1 oz raisins

20g / 1 oz pistachios, plus some extra for garnish

20g / 1 oz almonds, chopped

This dish is a famous traditional dessert in Egypt. It is usually cooked in the first month of the Islamic calendar. It is considered the quintessential Egyptian pudding.

Pumpkin Gratin

Serves: 2 – 4 | Preparation time: 1 hour, 30 minutes

1. Preheat oven to 160°C / 320°F.
2. Peel the pumpkin, and cut into slices. Remove the seeds.
3. Cook the pumpkin with butter and ¼ cup sugar in a deep pan, covered, on low heat, for 1 hour, until cooked through. You will notice that it releases juices, which will be reabsorbed as it cooks.
4. In another deep pan, make a béchamel: heat and combine the butter and flour to make a roux; on medium heat, add the milk gradually, stirring with a whisk; add the vanilla and the custard to thicken.
5. Stir well, gradually add ¼ cup of sugar, and stir over low heat for 5 minutes, then set aside.
6. Put half of the pumpkin in a *tagin*, add the mixed nuts in the center, and add the final layer of pumpkin.
7. Pour the béchamel on top.
8. Add a final layer of the heavy cream.
9. Bake in the oven for 15 minutes until the top turns light brown.

Can be served hot or cold.

1 small pumpkin (about 2kg / 4 lb)

4 tbsp butter

2 tbsp flour

250g / ½ cup sugar

250 ml / 1 cup milk

2 tbsp custard powder

200g / 7 oz almonds

200g / 7 oz raisins

200g / 7 oz hazelnuts

100g / ½ cup heavy cream

1 packet vanilla powder

This dish, pumpkin pudding, is one of the classic Egyptian desserts. It is best with a firm, ripe pumpkin. It is cooked and served in a tagin.

Index

Egyptian Authentic Restaurant

www.**abouelsid**.com